Wandering mind unfolds

Dolly Jayakrishnan

Presentation by *BookLeaf Publishing*

Web: www.bookleafpub.com

E-mail: info@bookleafpub.com

ISBN: 9789358366570

First edition 2023

Dedicated

to all those who love to dream...

to all those who believe in magic &
fairytales...

to all those who can hear the whispering of
the stars...

to all those who leave a li'l sparkle
wherever they go...

This is for YOU!

Never dying thoughts

In the story of my life,
The best chapters are filled with hers.
As far as I remember
She was the one who was not a stranger,
Someone who was simply down-to-earth and
sweet,
Someone who was always a treat.
She added rhythm to my heartbeats.
But alas, she was snatched away in a sudden,
Leaving me lost and depressed.
And after that, never was I under the shade,
The shade that gave me comfort, peace and
love.
It was hard to bear the loneliness,
The loneliness ended up as my only companion.
But her thoughts kept me alive,
Without which I couldn't survive.
If there was a way I could edit the past,
She would have been there
Beside me till the last.
But I know she's still up in the sky,
As a dazzling star, whispering to me, " I love
you, My daughter."
The whisper that keeps my heart going.
I'm still living in deep broken pain,
Waiting all alone to meet her one day…
Someday!

The Fall

Leaves disguise flowers
In vibrant red, gold and brown
Permeating joy in everyone.
Soon they die,
Swirling, twirling, falling down.
Yet with peace, and a smile,
Bidding all a goodbye,
Waiting to be born again someday!

You

The touch of your hand,
The warmth of your embrace,
A soft kiss on my head,
A touch that awakens the core of my soul,
The passion that binds in your grasp,
The feeling of oneness
where we fall into the same rhythm
feeling our unconditional love.
I love the way you are,
You're the one who completes me.
The look, the touch, the feel,
The passion in your eyes,
The purity of your soul,
The caress of your hands skips a beat of my
heart.
You are the one I want to love,
I want to spend an eternity with you!

My love

Loving you is a relief,
Feeling you is a belief.
My life is all about you,
Nothing more I could do.
When I breathe,
I have you in it.
When away, just feel,
I can't be without you a bit.
I try not to sway,
But can't find a way!

My giggle

I love you more than words can say,
But I'm going to try it anyway.
Even before you were born,
You stole my heart
And I knew that we would never depart!
You came into my life with a bundle of joy,
You will always be my baby boy.
You are my giggle,
You are my wiggle,
Loving you is my life,
Keep you safe from strife.
You are a gift beyond measure,
You are my most precious treasure!

Wounded heart

I want to scream out loud,
Throw out all the words
That I had to swallow
Once upon a time,
Squeeze out all the pain,
That froze my blood,
Heal the wounds,
Still bleeding in my heart!

I wish

I wish,
I wish,
I wish.
Though I know that
This wish of mine
Will always remain a wish,
But still,
I wish!

The beautiful pain

I feel the pain, I know the pain,
The pain I never knew before,
The feeling I never had before.
The pain of missing you,
The strain of being alone.
The feeling I just can't bear,
The meaning of life we share.

You were beside me always,
Beside me, when I cried;
To console me.
Beside me, when I was sad;
Feeling really bad.
Beside me, when I laughed;
Feeling really glad.
Beside me, when I gave up;
Asking me to try,
Never to you, I had the guts to lie.
Beside me, when I was in a dream;
Along with you, we were a team,
Still I feel you beside me;
Within me, around me, every time.

My eyes fill with tears,
My heart overflows with fears,

Facing life alone.
The thought tortures my mind,
I don't know why
I have more reasons to find.
I can't let myself away,
I see myself lost in you, today;
Something I can never deny
Because I just can't lie.
I can't retrieve myself back
There's something in me, I lack,
Like a baby in the darkness, lost
Searching for its guardian,
Who it loves the most.

This feeling I never had before,
I tell you, from my heart, for sure;
I have to share this with you, more.
The memories, the treasures that I wish to store,
You are the one, the only one, I adore.

I don't know where to start,
If we could rewind our past;
I tell you from the bottom of my heart,
I would like to live the story again,
The story that we together began.

I do believe in fate
At times fate is something I really hate,
Lemme tell you before it gets really late,

I really don't know
What you are to me.
I search my heart
If I could ever see,
What you are to me.

Being with you is the greatest wish
Loving you is the greatest gift,
The love that cannot be measured
The love that is to be treasured,
The love that can never be replaced
Our true love, the versatile love
Forever love!

Your love keeps me alive,
That drags me to survive,
The love that stays within two souls,
The love that never dies,
The love that took us to the skies,
That love that can never be washed away
By the waves of destiny!

Wonder how people change with no love

In the world of mankind,
Where can we find them being kind?
In this corrupted world,
Where people take advantage of others,
Where being cunning, people cheat
Acting very friendly and sweet.
Though I kept forgiving some,
Didn't learn a lesson from them.
All because of the love for the ones
Who never knows love.

Living with a wounded heart,
She comes into my life.
Should I call it fate
Or a disaster coming into my life?
I kept her more than a friend,
Sharing everything.
Forgetting my happiness,
Gave her everything to find her happiness
She was my princess,
I made sure others saw her that way.
Who could show such love these days?

I did love her in many ways.

I thought I was getting the same from her.
Love is blind, never knew what she was,
Though others kept warning
Don't regret the love you are shredding.
Sooner I knew what she was
The one among the corrupted world.
I learned that along,
The time which it proved so.

Still, before the blame I put on her,
I implored if I made a mistake to her.
For the sake of my love,
She just said that it was her fault.
I could have been happy with this answer,
But I couldn't find that in her eyes,
It was so filled with lies.
Deep in her eyes, there was no love.

I was not blind anymore.
The love that once made me blind,
The love that I didn't hide,
The love in her that I couldn't find,
The love that she didn't mind.
Still, I tried to be a better person,
Yet she neglected, ignored, and insulted.

Is it because she achieved heights or desires in
life?
Is it because I was no longer required in her life?

Or is it because of the effect of all evil eyes,
Though not true, it could cover up all the lies.
Or is it because she never loved me?
The pain in my heart stays throughout my life.
I still wonder how people change with no love!

Beach

The warmth of the sun,
The blowing wind,
The soft white sand,
The sound of the waves
Crashing on the shore,
The soothing noise
Makes me fall in love
The feeling, still unknown.
The aqua blue sea,
Mesmerizes me.
Sand between my toes,
And my wet summer clothes,
The aroma of seafood,
Fills my nose.
The funnel cakes so tempting, you see
And the seagulls flying above me.
The pebbles and seashells
Brings out the child in me.
I close my eyes,
And I am at peace
"This is my happy place"
I say, with a smiling face,
Surrounded by the positive vibe,
I wish the waves would carry me
to another world,

Being in total awe when I see
The new world of fantasy
Where mermaids and fairies are so real.
I wonder if it's a mystery,
I fall in love with the sea.
Where I wish I could always be
A feeling of Harmony!

My world, You are

There's no way I can articulate
What you mean to me
Can't just express
The joy you brought in me,
You brought out the real me in me
A second with you
Is a dream come true!

Your thoughts make my nights sleepless,
Yet at the same time lulls to sleep-
With a warm caress.
You are the one who comes in all my dreams-
Fondling your fingers over me
Like the waves dancing with the rhythm of the
seas,
Which makes me feel like lullabies
You are the song of my heart
Promise me, we won't ever depart
No matter what,
Together we were meant to be.
You mean the world to me!

Anxiety

A N X I E T Y
I don't know why I listen to YOU,
I wish I could expose YOU,
YOU are the little voice inside my head
things I can't talk about,
For fear, I'll forget
Who I am and change into YOU.

YOU are
The Panic,
The worry,
The Threat,
The darkness to my world.

Tightness in my chest,
I struggle to breathe,
My heart goes pounding,
My head starts spinning,
My body starts trembling,
My hands start to shake,
I can feel the horrible heartache.
A lump in my throat,
Can't just swallow,
My mind goes hollow,
Can't bear the pain.

I can't stop crying,
It feels like I'm dying.

"Breathe. You will get through this"
I hear voices around
and I scream back loud
"Grab my hand, please don't let me go!"
ANXIETY, I'm done with YOU!
I had enough,
Enough of YOU!
Take me away
Or leave me alone!
Enough! I can't take this anymore.
Why does this come to me, OH God!

The weird old man

I remember seeing this old man
In my dreams, when I was a child.
I don't know who he was.
He was the one-
Limbing towards me,
His clothes torn,
All dirty brown.
Wrinkles all over his face,
His crooked look.
His eyes, wide open
Creepy and red,
As red as blood.
I knew he was a threat,
He was a psychopath
With a knife in his blood-stained arm,
I was sure he was about to harm.
Though I try to take my eyes off him,
I am stuck in the sequence of
Black and white spirals revolving around him.
Was he trying to hypnotize me?
The spirals are coming closer, I see.
I close my eyes as hard as I can,
Darkness creeps into my soul
And my heart,
I am not even able to react.

I can hardly speak or scream aloud,
I see myself all alone.
I finally wake up from my nap,
And made my way out of his trap.
I wonder why is he stuck in my head for years,
I wish someday he disappears.
Every night fear shakes me awake,
Though I am well aware
He is just a nightmare!

Memories

Each day that passes by,
A memory it leaves behind.
Good ones, I treasure forever,
And the bad ones, I would never.
Those memories that linger and last,
Those moments vanished so fast,
If ever I'm feeling sad or low,
I will pick that moment from my heart.
The moment that I would always love to cherish,
And I'm sure I would have that smile,
The smile that makes me forget all my pain,
Days, months, or years may pass by,
But I would always remain the same.
Within me will be the cute memories,
Which will always last
forever and Forever!

Rain

The rhythm of the rain
As they splash on the ground,
I love to hear
Their mellifluous sound.
The smell of the rain,
The petrichor,
I love the feeling,
The power of my soul healing.
I am in love with the rain,
It's like stroking my brain.
The air is cool and fresh,
I wish in the rain, I could drench.
I love being in the rain,
I walk beside the lane,
My clothes soaked and wet,
I feel so good, you bet!

The fire in me

The fire in me,
The burning pain,
The sensation I feel,
A spark that grew
From deep within.

The fire in me,
Keeps burning for long.
It's not docile until
The silence of ferocity
Are completely gone.

The fire in me,
Burning to be let out,
I sparge the flame,
Stopping it from getting out.

The fire in me,
Impossible to ignore.
At times I believe
It might be all gone.

I wish the fire in me
Could burn my tears
Into ashes,

That's what I feel
Or else I will never heal.

Sunflower

I want to be a sunflower,
Following the sun's rays,
Throughout the days.
Glowing bright
Like a fire
In Flaming yellow,
And the hues of gold,
The tales untold.
Standing up tall,
Even after I fall,
Always holding my head up high
To chase the sky,
Until I die!

Depression

Depression is not fun,
It's not a shame,
Society thinks it's a disgrace.
They are forced to hide,
For the sake of prestige,
Rather than help the affected ones in need.
It's just another disease,
Which is hard to cease.
But an illness that affects
The mind,
And which is hard
To find.
Trust me, peace of mind
Is all what I need.
It's easy to find fault
When I really need support.
But the real pain is
The fear that if I'm insane.
I search deep within me,
If there is any joy I could find.
Someday I wish I could see
The happy version of ME.

Flowers in my heart

27

I've learned to grow flowers
In the wounded parts
of my heart,
If the light ever penetrates,
It would know where to start.
To start from the memories,
That died a long time ago,
My fears,
My tears and
These years
Taught me this art,
The rejuvenation of my heart.

Kids

I love kids
With all my heart,
Their innocence, their giggles,
Their art.
Their boundless energy,
They are a bundle of joy.
Their mischievous act,
They never annoy.

Their smile can light up the darkest day,
Their hugs can chase the blues away.
Their curious minds, full of wonder,
Sometimes makes me surrender.

With kids, every moment is an adventure,
A journey of discovery, a joyful chapter.
Their creativity knows no bounds,
Their imagination forever astounds.

Let us nurture
And guide them well,
So they can grow,
And their dreams can swell.

Living in a dream

If you are a dream
Don't wake me up
Lemme sleep forever-
So that we can be together,
F O R E V E R!

If you are a dream,
Then let me never leave,
For in your eyes,
All my fears relieve.

If you are a dream,
Then let me never awake,
For in your presence
All my troubles flake.

Your voice is the music
That soothes my soul,
In my life,
You play a major role.
With you by my side,
Never again, will I fall,
All my worries will resolve!